our
Environment

Pollution

Kris Hirschmann

KIDHAVEN PRESS
An imprint of Thomson Gale, a part of The Thomson Corporation

THOMSON
™
GALE

Detroit • New York • San Francisco • San Diego • New Haven, Conn.
Waterville, Maine • London • Munich

For more information, contact
KidHaven Press
27500 Drake Rd.
Farmington Hills, MI 48331-3535
Or you can visit our Internet site at http://www.gale.com

LIBRARY OF CONGRESS CATALOGING-IN-PUBLICATION DATA

Hirschmann, Kris.
  Pollution / by Kris Hirschmann.
    p. cm. — (Our environment)
  Contents: What is pollution?—Air pollution—Water pollution—Garbage.
  Includes bibliographical references and index.
  ISBN 0-7377-1563-4 (alk. paper)
  I. Title. II. Our environment.

contents

chapter one

What Is Pollution?

Pollution is anything released into earth's air or water or onto its land faster than earth can break it down. Although natural forces are always working to break down existing **pollutants**, new ones are being released so quickly that earth cannot always keep up. The result is that in many areas, earth today is suffering from pollution.

Quantity Matters

Some pollutants are not necessarily harmful in small doses. In fact, some are completely natural. A good example is carbon dioxide, a gas that is a normal part of the atmosphere. Carbon dioxide is also found naturally in the bodies of all people and animals, and plants "breathe" it in to survive in the same way that humans breathe oxygen. Yet in large amounts carbon dioxide can kill living creatures. Some scientists believe that too much of this gas might even change earth's climate over long periods.

Human waste is another natural substance that is harmless in small doses. This substance makes a good fertilizer for crops. It also **decomposes** (breaks down) easily when it is exposed to natural forces. But if

Chemicals, sewage, and trash pollute this river in Argentina, making it unsafe for people and animals.

human waste builds up too quickly, it can do damage. Too much waste can choke waterways, kill marine animals, and carry diseases that sicken or kill people.

Some pollutants are unsafe in any amount. The tiniest bit of radioactivity, for example, can make people and animals sick; larger amounts can kill.

Natural Sources of Pollution

Earth itself creates some types of pollution. Volcanoes are the most important source of natural pollution. When volcanoes erupt, they release plumes of ash, smoke, and poisonous gases into the air. These pollutants rise high into the sky, where they are carried around the globe by winds.

Major eruptions can spew enough pollution into the air to temporarily affect earth's climate. When a Mexican volcano called El Chichon erupted in 1982, for example, parts of earth's surface cooled down for a few years. This change happened because some of the sun's rays were blocked by pollutants high in the atmosphere.

Other natural sources of pollution include forest fires and dust storms. These events do not produce as many pollutants as volcanic eruptions do, but they can be harmful as well. In the year 2000, forest and grassland fires in Africa released gases and particles that eventually blew all the way to Australia. And in 2002, forest fires in the state of Colorado created enough carbon dioxide to raise levels of this gas around the world.

Astronauts in space took this photo of the clouds of smoke and ash erupting from Sicily's Mount Etna in 2002.

Human Sources of Pollution

Although some sources of pollution are natural, most pollution is caused by humans. Humans pollute in three main ways: through farming, industries, and cities.

Farming pollutes mostly through the use of chemicals, including **pesticides**, **fungicides**, and fertilizers. These chemicals seep into the soil, then wash into rivers, lakes, and streams. Waste from farm animals also causes pollution when rain flushes it into the water system. And soil **erosion** adds to the pollution problem as well. Plowing strips plants off earth's surface, leaving bare dirt that can blow into rivers and streams. This dirt clogs waterways and hurts plant and animal life.

Industries pollute in many ways. Factories release poisonous materials through smokestacks or underwater pipes. Dangerous gases include carbon monoxide, hydrocarbons, sulfur, and nitrogen oxides. Poisonous metals such as arsenic, lead, mercury, beryllium, and chromium are also released during some manufacturing processes.

Dangerous gases spew from the smokestacks of a plant that produce chemicals needed to make plastic.

These materials and others can damage both the environment and living creatures.

Human communities, especially large cities, are the last major source of pollution. Motor vehicles release carbon monoxide and other harmful gases into the air. Huge amounts of human waste must be disposed of. So must garbage, which is produced in large quantities wherever many people gather. And some appliances, including refrigerators, air conditioners, and light fixtures, contain substances that can pollute the air and water. These appliances often break when they are thrown away. This allows the pollutants inside to escape into the environment.

How Bad Is the Problem?

People are polluting the earth. But not everyone agrees about the seriousness of the problem. Some scientists, for example, believe that the world's rivers, lakes, streams, and oceans are much too polluted and likely to get worse. Others point out that thanks to today's regulations and cleanup efforts over the past few decades, these same bodies of water are much cleaner than they used to be. Similar arguments have been made for air pollution and garbage.

One of the most hotly debated pollution issues concerns the release of carbon dioxide gas into the atmosphere. Many scientists believe that this gas will "thicken" earth's atmosphere and trap extra heat from the sun. They think that over time this trapped heat will permanently raise earth's air temperature. This process is called **global warming**. Other scientists, however, do not feel that global warming is an issue. They agree that carbon dioxide levels are rising, but they do not think that earth will get warmer as a result.

Recycling is another confusing issue. Recycling is a program in which used goods such as paper, plastics, and glass are collected, then processed so they can be used again. Recycling reduces the amount of waste that becomes permanent pollution. However, recycling facilities use power, which comes from factories that produce air and water pollution. The trucks that carry used cans and newspapers to recycling facilities also create pollution. And recycling paper and some other materials actually uses more polluting chemicals than creating brand-new paper does. For these reasons and others, not everybody agrees that recycling is a good long-term solution.

The global warming and recycling debates, among others, show that pollution is not a clear-cut issue. There are many ways to interpret the information that is available today.

Can People Make a Difference?

Although the long-term effects of pollution are not clear, one thing is certain: Less pollution is better. Today people continue to find ways to reduce pollution.

One example of a clear improvement is the cleanup of factory waste. The smokestacks of many

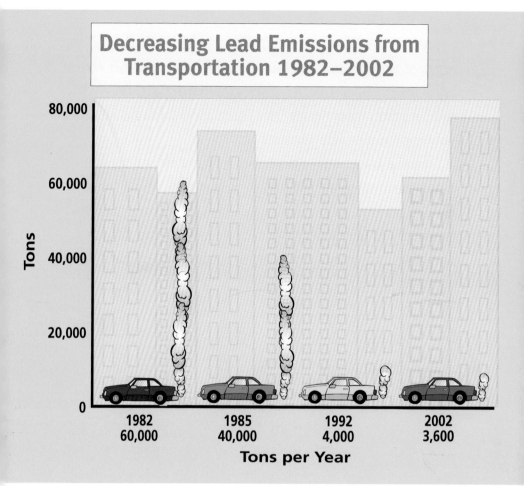

Decreasing Lead Emissions from Transportation 1982–2002

Tons

80,000

60,000

40,000

20,000

0

| 1982 | 1985 | 1992 | 2002 |
| 60,000 | 40,000 | 4,000 | 3,600 |

Tons per Year

factories now contain **scrubbers**, devices that re-move the worst pollutants from waste products. Some scrubbers are so efficient that they remove more than 98 percent of the **particulates** (tiny solid particles) from an airstream.

Another example is a change in the way gasoline is made. At one time all gasoline in the United States contained lead. When burned, the gasoline released lead particles into the air. These particles were breathed in by people. Lead was later shown to cause kidney and heart problems. It also affects the mental development of children. In the mid-1970s, laws were passed requiring all U.S. gasoline to be lead-free. As a result, airborne lead particles—and the health problems they cause—are no longer widespread in the United States.

These successes and others prove that human actions can make a difference. It is not possible to stop pollution entirely. Through laws and everyday behaviors, however, people can have a big effect on the amount of pollution that is created.

chapter two

Air Pollution

Air pollution occurs when certain gases, liquid droplets, or particulates are released into the atmosphere. There are many sources of air pollution, including the exhaust from motor vehicles, factory smokestacks, and the burning of trash and other materials.

Most human-created air pollution comes from burning fossil fuels. Fossil fuels include coal, gasoline, and oil. When these substances burn, they release poisonous gases such as carbon monoxide and nitrogen oxides. They also release dust, soot, and other particulates. All of these materials enter the atmosphere, where they linger as pollution.

Most air pollution is created in and around cities. But because wind can carry pollutants thousands of miles from their sources, unpopulated areas sometimes suffer from air pollution too.

Smog

Air pollution near cities is usually called **smog**. The most common type is called **photochemical smog**. It is created when the exhaust from motor vehicles reacts with sunlight to form a chemical called ozone. Other substances in the exhaust join into droplets, creating a brown haze. This ozone-rich haze makes it hard for people to breathe, and it can also hurt people's eyes. Coughing, sneezing, and nausea are other common reactions to photochemical smog.

Exhaust from motor vehicles reacts with sunlight to create a brown haze of smog over downtown Los Angeles.

In most areas wind scatters smog. A few cities, however, are located in places where geography and climate trap smog instead of carrying it away. Los Angeles, California, and Denver, Colorado, are two such cities in the United States. Milan, Italy; Mexico City, Mexico; Tokyo, Japan; and Buenos Aires, Brazil, are a few other cities around the world that struggle with smog.

Acid Rain

Acid rain is another problem created by air pollution. Acid rain gets its start when factories and motor vehicles release sulfur dioxide and nitrogen oxides. In the air these gases react with wind, sunlight, water vapor, and oxygen to form acids. The acid droplets float on air currents for days or even weeks. Rain or snow eventually pick them up and carry them to the ground.

Acid rain is most common in the eastern United States and Canada. The source of the pollution in this region is factories in Canada, West Virginia, Pennsylvania, and some midwestern U.S. states. Factories elsewhere in the world create acid rain that affects parts of Scandinavia, China, Japan, Russia, and South America.

Acid rain can kill all living things in a lake. When acid rain falls into a lake over a long period, fish, clams, and other lake animals begin to die. Insects that lay their eggs in or on the water die too, as do underwater plants. If the acid content of the lake

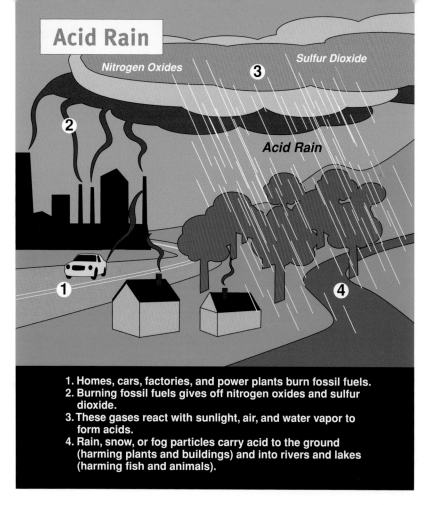

Acid Rain

Nitrogen Oxides

Sulfur Dioxide

③

②

Acid Rain

①

④

1. Homes, cars, factories, and power plants burn fossil fuels.
2. Burning fossil fuels gives off nitrogen oxides and sulfur dioxide.
3. These gases react with sunlight, air, and water vapor to form acids.
4. Rain, snow, or fog particles carry acid to the ground (harming plants and buildings) and into rivers and lakes (harming fish and animals).

rises high enough, all plant and animal life will disappear. A small percentage (less than 10 percent) of the lakes in Scandinavia, eastern Canada, and New York State qualify as "dead" lakes.

Acid may also harm trees. Some scientists believe that acidic fog around certain mountain areas, such as New York's Adirondack Mountains and Vermont's Green Mountains, damage the leaves and bark of trees. Over time this fog may weaken the trees so much that they fall prey to insects or disease. It is very hard, however, to tell the difference between damage caused by acid fog and damage from other causes. For this reason it is difficult to know how bad the acid fog problem really is.

Yet another effect of acid rain is damage to buildings and structures. For example, the walls of the U.S. Capitol in Washington, D.C., are covered with tiny holes where acid has eaten into the stone. And marble monuments in some cemeteries are so acid-etched that their words can no longer be read.

Scientists disagree about acid rain. Some feel it is a major problem that demands

A forest in Tennessee and a stone sculpture from a French church (inset) show the severe damage acid rain causes.

solutions. Others point out that even in the worst affected areas, only 4 to 5 percent of all lakes are severely acidified. Recent studies also show that rain is less acidic now than it was in the 1970s and 1980s. As a result, lakes and streams in many areas are becoming less acidic as well. This change is probably due to regulations that were put in place between 1970 and 1990. Factories today give off less sulfur dioxide and nitrogen oxides than they once did, so less acid rain is created.

Climatic Changes

Some scientists believe that air pollution could permanently change earth's climate. A major issue is global warming. In the past hundred years, earth's average air temperature has risen about one degree Fahrenheit. Continued change could lead to thawing permafrost (frozen ground) in polar areas, rising sea levels, and warmer ocean temperatures, all of which would be harmful to humans. If carbon dioxide is causing earth's temperature to rise, it makes sense to get this form of pollution under control immediately. But is carbon dioxide pollution truly responsible? No one knows for sure. Earth warms and cools naturally over long periods of time. Many scientists believe that earth is now in a natural warming period. Neither carbon dioxide nor any other form of air pollution, they say, has anything to do with this trend.

Another concern is the thinning of the **ozone layer**. The ozone layer is a thick blanket of gas that

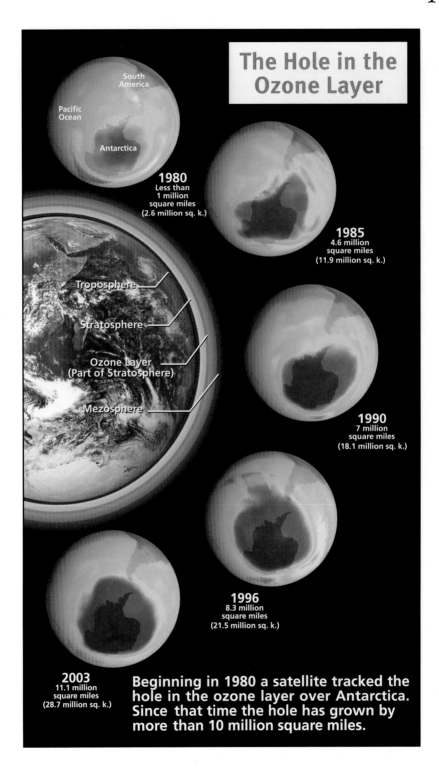

The Hole in the Ozone Layer

South America
Pacific Ocean
Antarctica

1980
Less than
1 million
square miles
(2.6 million sq. k.)

1985
4.6 million
square miles
(11.9 million sq. k.)

Troposphere
Stratosphere
Ozone Layer
(Part of Stratosphere)
Mezosphere

1990
7 million
square miles
(18.1 million sq. k.)

1996
8.3 million
square miles
(21.5 million sq. k.)

2003
11.1 million
square miles
(28.7 million sq. k.)

Beginning in 1980 a satellite tracked the
hole in the ozone layer over Antarctica.
Since that time the hole has grown by
more than 10 million square miles.

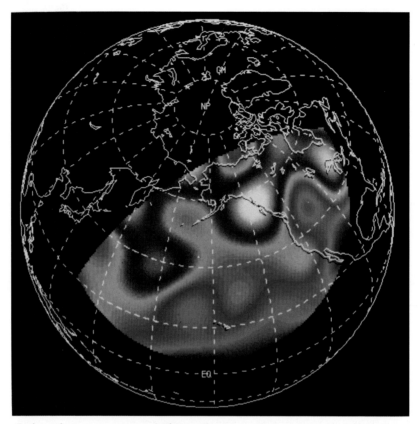

Scientists use special equipment to measure ozone levels in earth's atmosphere. In this image, the red areas show where ozone levels are low.

floats between ten and thirty miles (16–48 kilometers) above earth's surface. At ground level, ozone is harmful to life. In earth's atmosphere, however, this gas protects life by absorbing dangerous radiation from the sun. Without ozone, earth would be nothing but a hot rock where no plants or animals could survive.

In the 1980s scientists discovered that pollutants from earth's surface were rising all the way to the ozone layer. Once there, the pollutants were destroying ozone, especially over the Antarctic. As a result, people who lived in New Zealand, Australia, Argentina, Chile, and other regions near the Antarctic began to develop cancer at higher rates than did people in other parts of the world. This trend continues to the present day.

Taking Action

People around the world are taking action to reduce air pollution. One important agreement is the Montreal Protocol on Substances that Deplete the Ozone Layer. Countries that signed this 1987 treaty pledged to reduce their production and use of **chlorofluorocarbons** (CFCs), a type of pollutant that is especially damaging to the ozone layer. They also agreed to cut back on the production of other ozone-harming substances. Today more than 180 countries have signed the Montreal Protocol. The U.S. Environmental Protection Agency (EPA) believes that the ozone layer could recover fully by the year 2050 if people stop releasing ozone-depleting substances.

In the United States another important step toward reducing air pollution has been the Clean Air Act of 1970. This act allows the EPA to set national standards for air quality. Each state then has to make sure the air within its borders meets these standards. States do this by issuing permits to factories and inspecting them to make sure they are "clean," monitoring the air quality in cities, and more. The Clean Air Act and others like it around the world have already reduced air pollution in many areas, and they will continue to make a difference in years to come.

chapter three

Water Pollution

Water pollution begins when damaging substances find their way into lakes, streams, rivers, or oceans. These substances may settle to the bottom, or they may float within the water.

Water pollution has many sources. Garbage dumping plays a role. So does air pollution, which sometimes falls into waterways. Soil erosion can also pollute rivers and lakes.

Most water pollution, however, is caused by **sewage**. There are three types of sewage: domestic sewage (wastewater from human homes), industrial sewage (wastewater from industrial facilities), and storm sewage (also called **runoff**).

Domestic Sewage

Domestic sewage is used water from people's toilets, showers, and sinks. This water contains human waste products, food scraps, household chemicals, and other damaging substances.

Domestic sewage carries a tiny amount of pollutants—less than 0.1 percent by weight. However, these pollutants are dangerous because they can carry diseases. One example is typhoid fever, which strikes about 17 million people and kills 600,000

A pipe dumps sewage directly into India's Ganges River. The Ganges is one of the world's most polluted rivers.

each year worldwide. This disease is rare in countries where **sanitation** is good. In countries where human sewage flows directly into public waterways, however, diseases like typhoid are an ongoing problem. In Bangladesh, for instance, people living along the highly polluted Ganges River are often struck by typhoid and other waterborne illnesses.

Domestic sewage can also damage underwater life. In the Caribbean, for example, a disease called white pox is destroying coral reefs. This disease is caused by a germ that is usually found in the human intestine.

This paper mill in Spain produces toxic by-products called dioxins that can make their way into nearby water supplies.

Scientists think that the germ probably entered the oceans through the release of untreated waste.

In developed countries steps are taken to make sure domestic sewage does not become a major problem. Sewage usually passes through water treatment plants, where it is processed to remove all harmful bacteria and most other pollutants. The treated water is then disinfected before being released into the environment. It is not completely free of pollutants, but it is clean enough to support underwater life. People can also swim in treated water without fear of getting sick.

Industrial Sewage

Industrial sewage is used water from manufacturing processes. Industries have several ways to get rid of this water. They may release it into special holding ponds. They may cause it to evaporate. Or they may simply dump it into rivers through underwater pipes. The dumping of untreated industrial sewage is against the law in most developed countries. In many developing countries, however, it is not. Mexico and India, for example, have water pollution problems stemming from industrial sewage.

The pollutants in industrial sewage are usually chemicals or metals. These substances are either used in manufacturing processes or are created during those processes. One example is a group of chemicals called **dioxins**. These pollutants are created by many industries, including pulp mills (factories that turn wood into the raw materials needed to make paper). Pulp mills use chlorine compounds to bleach wood fibers. The process makes dioxins, some of which are released into waterways.

In the United States, dioxin release is controlled by the National Pollutant Discharge Elimination System (NPDES). Under this program, pulp mills and other dioxin-producing industries must get permits showing that the pollutant level in their discharges is below acceptable levels. Established in 1990, the NPDES has been a big help in reducing waterborne dioxins.

Storm Sewage

Storm sewage, or runoff, is created when it rains. Rainwater absorbs pollution from the ground, then trickles into sewers or waterways. Runoff that enters sewer systems can be treated to remove pollutants. Runoff that flows directly into waterways cannot be treated.

Farms are a major source of runoff. Rainwater that falls in farm areas becomes polluted with fertilizers, pesticides, and other chemicals used on soil and crops, as well as waste products from farm animals. The polluted rainwater eventually reaches rivers, lakes, and other bodies of water. In 2000, 19 percent of America's rivers were examined for pollution. Of these, 39 percent were found to be polluted. Experts estimate that just over half of the pollutants in these rivers came from agricultural runoff.

Cities are another primary source of runoff. City streets and parking lots are covered with garbage and waste products from motor vehicles. Houses and buildings are coated with soot, smoke, and other pollutants. And sewage from people's septic tanks bubbles through the soil in many places. After a hard rain, these pollutants and others are washed into waterways and oceans.

Effects of Water Pollution

Domestic, industrial, and storm sewage have many effects on underwater environments. One of these effects is called **eutrophication**. Eutrophication is a

Waterways near livestock farms like this one are often polluted by the runoff from large amounts of animal waste.

This pond is overgrown with green algae (close-up, inset), a microscopic organism that quickly multiplies in polluted waters.

natural step in the aging cycle of lakes. Pollution, however, dramatically speeds up the process.

When organic wastes and fertilizers get dumped into lakes, they encourage the growth of algae, small water plants. The algae grow out of control until they begin to choke the lake. Then the algae die and start to decay. The decaying algae reduce the level of oxygen in the water, which kills fish and plants. At the same time, the algae are eaten by bacteria that release bad-smelling gases. Soon a once clear body of water has turned into a dead, stinking mass.

Today eutrophication is considered the biggest water pollution issue around the world. It can be seen in lakes everywhere, and many rivers are also affected. Its effects, however, are limited. Eutrophication happens mostly in very polluted areas around cities or big factories. Widespread eutrophication is not nearly as common. But it does occur in a few places, including Lake Erie and the Baltic Sea.

Toxic Buildup

Another effect of water pollution is **toxic buildup**. Toxic buildup occurs when certain substances, such as DDT (a pesticide) and mercury, are released into waterways. These substances settle to the bottom, where they coat plants. The plants are eaten by small fish, which may be eaten by larger fish. As the chemicals move up the food chain, they become more and more concentrated in animals' flesh. At some point they start to do harm. Different toxins may affect animals' behavior, immune systems, or ability to reproduce.

Sometimes people get sick after eating contaminated fish. Major poisoning incidents are rare, but they do happen occasionally. More often, however, people just absorb the toxins and store them harmlessly in their fat. Mercury and **polychlorinated biphenyls** (PCBs) are two pollutants often carried by fish and eaten in tiny amounts by humans.

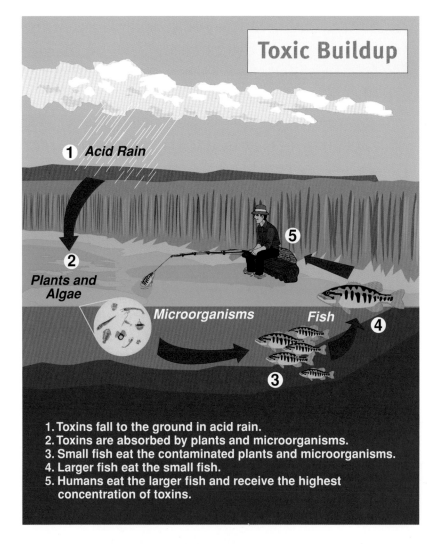

Toxic Buildup

1 *Acid Rain*

2
Plants and Algae

5

Microorganisms

Fish

4

3

1. Toxins fall to the ground in acid rain.
2. Toxins are absorbed by plants and microorganisms.
3. Small fish eat the contaminated plants and microorganisms.
4. Larger fish eat the small fish.
5. Humans eat the larger fish and receive the highest concentration of toxins.

Cleaning Up the World's Waters

Water pollution in developed countries is not as bad today as it was just a few decades ago. People now realize how much harm they can do by dumping sewage and other untreated pollutants into waterways. As a result many governments have passed laws to prevent this from happening. In the United States, the two main laws that regulate water pollution are the Safe Drinking Water Act (1974) and the Clean Water Act (1977). These laws limit the amount of pollutants allowed in public waterways and drinking water. States must make sure their water meets the standards described in these laws.

Not all countries regulate water pollution. Many developing nations cannot afford good public sanitation systems. In these countries sewage and other pollutants are still released directly into the water. In other countries factories are allowed to pour untreated wastewater into rivers. And regions all over the world suffer from accidental oil spills, sewage dumping from ships, and other unregulated pollution sources. Most of these problems can be brought under control if people take action. The sooner they do, the sooner earth's most polluted waters can begin to heal.

Chapter Four

Garbage

People do not just pollute earth's air and water. They also litter the land with garbage—unwanted materials such as paper, plastics, metals, wood, and food scraps. In developed countries each person produces several pounds of garbage per day.

In the United States paper and cardboard products make up about 40 percent of the weight of city garbage. Food waste accounts for about 10 percent of the garbage. The rest is a mixture of yard trimmings, wood, glass, metal, plastic, leather, cloth, and other materials.

Getting Rid of Garbage

Garbage builds up very quickly near homes and businesses. Since garbage usually contains smelly and germ-filled food waste, it must be removed quickly. In most areas this task is handled by garbage trucks. The trucks have built-in crushers that smash garbage to less than half its original volume. By doing this, garbage trucks can gather more trash before dumping their loads.

Once garbage has been collected, it may be treated to make it smaller. The most common way of doing this is through **incineration**, or burning. Incineration turns garbage into a mixture of ash and solid chunks of metal, glass, and other hard-to-burn materials. When the burning process is finished, garbage weighs only about 10 percent as much as it did originally.

Another way to reduce the size of garbage is through **composting**. In this method, organic waste

An incinerator burns garbage to reduce its size, but the process releases ash and other pollutants into the air.

(including food scraps, lawn trimmings, and wood) is separated from glass, metal, and other inorganic materials. The organic waste is shredded to form a fine debris. This debris is then stored in piles and stirred every few days. Within a few weeks bacteria within the debris have digested the waste. The leftover material is called compost. It is a safe, clean mixture that can be sold as mulch or soil fertilizer.

Not all garbage receives size-reduction treatments. Most is taken directly to sanitary landfills, which are safe dumping grounds for trash. Sanitary landfills

Earthworms are often used to break down food scraps, lawn clippings, and other organic material into compost.

have special liners that keep waste from touching underground or surface water. Also, they are covered each day with a fresh layer of soil that traps smells and discourages bugs and rodents. These measures and others stop landfill garbage from polluting air or water or becoming a health hazard.

How Well Does It Work?

All methods of garbage disposal have good and bad points. Incineration, for example, is an excellent way to shrink garbage volume. The small amount of ash and debris that remains after garbage burns takes up very little room in a landfill. However, incineration also releases many pollutants, including dangerous gases, cinders, dust, and soot. For this reason garbage must be burned in special furnaces that trap pollutants. These furnaces are expensive to build and operate. They also use a great deal of electricity—and creating electricity usually involves the burning of fossil fuels, which creates air pollution.

Composting, too, has pros and cons. On the positive side, it changes garbage into something that is actually useful to the environment. On the negative side, composting only works for organic material, which makes up just a small part of the garbage created. Also, finished compost can be hard to get rid of. Compost is a good natural fertilizer, but it is heavy and therefore expensive to ship. For this reason many farmers prefer chemical fertilizers and will not buy compost.

Finally, landfills have many good and bad points. Landfills are the safest places to store most types of garbage. They are also inexpensive to build and operate, and they can handle a lot of trash in a small amount of space. On the other hand, landfills take up valuable land near cities. They also produce methane, a poisonous gas that must be carefully controlled. And they can leak a pollutant called **leachate** if they are not well built. Leachate is created when water enters a landfill and picks up dangerous substances produced by decomposing garbage.

Serious problems, however, are extremely rare at modern facilities. Today's landfills are so sturdy that pollutants rarely escape. Abandoned and covered-over landfills are considered so safe, in fact, that sometimes they are made into public recreation areas.

Hazardous Waste

Some garbage is too dangerous to be handled using normal methods. Garbage that requires special treatment or disposal is called **hazardous waste**.

There are many reasons a material might be considered hazardous. It could be poisonous, causing illness or even death if it comes into contact with people or animals. It could burn or explode easily. It could cause chemical reactions that destroy solid materials and living tissue on contact. It could carry diseases. It could even be radioactive.

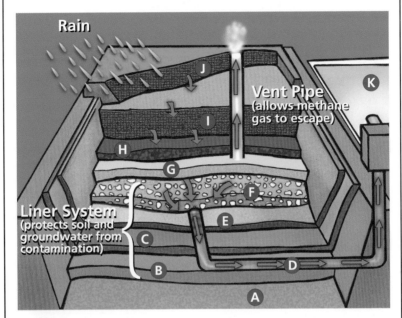

A Sanitary Landfill

Rain

Vent Pipe
(allows methane
gas to escape)

Liner System
(protects soil and
groundwater from
contamination)

- **A** Groundwater
- **B** Compacted Clay
- **C** Plastic Liner
- **D** Leachate Collection Pipe
- **E** Geotextile Mat
- **F** Gravel
- **G** Drainage Layer
- **H** Soil Layer
- **I** Old Trash
- **J** New Trash
- **K** Leachate Pond (contaminated water)

Garbage that meets any of these conditions must be handled very carefully.

Some types of hazardous waste can be incinerated. Other types cannot be destroyed, but they can be contained to make them safer. Some hazardous waste is sealed into concrete or plastic to keep it from touching soil, air, or water. Other waste is mixed with ash, water, and other materials to create cementlike blocks. Pollutants that are trapped within these blocks will not escape into the environment if the blocks are handled safely.

Once hazardous waste has been treated, it must be stored. Secure landfills are the most commonly

Wearing protective clothing and masks, workers clean up hazardous waste that accidentally spilled on a roadway.

used storage method. Secure landfills are a lot like sanitary landfills, but they are built to much stricter safety standards. They also include pollution detection systems that warn operators if dangerous substances are escaping. If leaks are detected, people can take action right away to correct the problem.

Secure landfills and other hazardous-waste disposal systems work well when they are used properly. However, the disposal of hazardous waste is a recent science. Unsafe dumping grounds that were used just a few decades ago have severely polluted the soil and water in some areas. People who are exposed to the pollutants in these areas may experience nausea, headaches, breathing problems, heart trouble, and birth defects. People may also develop cancer after being exposed to hazardous waste.

What Is Being Done?

In the United States, the government is working to clean up hazardous waste sites. Money for the cleanup comes from a 1980 law called the Comprehensive Environmental Response, Compensation, and Liability Act. This law is nicknamed "**Superfund**." Areas that qualify for cleanup under this law are called Superfund sites. Today there are thousands of Superfund sites, and many more will eventually be added to the list. With continued effort, people should be able to improve the soil and water quality in these areas.

Action is also being taken to cut down on every-day garbage. For example, industries are doing their part by developing lighter packaging. A two-liter plastic bottle, for instance, today weighs about two-thirds what it did in the 1970s, and a plastic grocery sack weighs only about one-third as much. Lighter packaging means less material to clutter landfills.

People everywhere can help as well by buying fewer items that will end up as garbage. If they do buy garbage-producing items, they should try to use them more than once. For example, an empty plastic water bottle might be refilled from the tap rather than thrown away. By taking these simple steps, anybody can take positive action to reduce garbage pollution.

Glossary

acid rain: Rain that is polluted with acid.

chlorofluorocarbons: Chemicals made by mixing chlorine, fluorine, and carbon. Chlorofluorocarbons destroy ozone.

composting: Storing organic waste in a way that makes it decay into harmless material.

decompose: To break down naturally over time.

dioxins: Pollutants created when pulp mills bleach wood products.

erosion: The removal of topsoil by wind, water, and other natural forces.

eutrophication: A process by which a body of water loses its oxygen after becoming choked with plant growth.

fungicides: Chemicals that kill fungi.

global warming: An increase in average world temperatures caused by the buildup of carbon dioxide.

hazardous waste: Dangerous garbage that requires special treatment or disposal.

incineration: Burning.

leachate: Polluted water that leaks from landfills.

ozone layer: A radiation-absorbing blanket of gas that surrounds the earth.

particulates: Tiny solid particles.

pesticides: Chemicals that kill insects and other animals that are considered to be pests.

photochemical smog: A type of smog that is produced when sunlight reacts with motor vehicle exhaust.

pollution: Anything that is released into earth's air or water or onto its land faster than earth can break it down.

pollutants: Substances that have the potential to cause pollution.

polychlorinated biphenyls (PCBs): Mixtures of chlorinated compounds. PCBs may be solids, liquids, or vapors.

recycling: Processing used goods so they can be reused.

runoff: Rainwater that hits the land, then flows into bodies of water.

sanitation: Systems that process waste to keep the environment clean and healthy.

scrubbers: Devices inside factory smokestacks that remove pollutants from dirty air.

sewage: Polluted water from human homes, industries, or storm runoff.

smog: The name given to air pollution near cities.

Superfund: A law that provides money to clean up hazardous waste sites.

toxic buildup: When dangerous pollutants gather in animals' flesh.

For Further Exploration

Books

Molly Garrett Bang, *Chattanooga Sludge: Cleaning Toxic Sludge from Chattanooga Creek.* San Diego, CA: Harcourt Brace, 1996. The author explains the efforts to clean up Tennessee's Chattanooga Creek, badly polluted by years of industrial dumping.

Rob Bowden, *Waste, Recycling, and Reuse: Our Impact on the Planet.* Austin, TX: Raintree Steck-Vaughn, 2002. Discusses types of waste, disposal methods, costs, and what can be done about the problem of waste.

Mark Maslin, *Global Warming: Causes, Effects, and the Future.* Stillwater, MN: Voyageur, 2002. An easy-to-understand summary of global warming and the debates surrounding this issue.

Louise Petheram, *Acid Rain.* Mankato, MN: Bridgestone Books, 2003. A good explanation of acid rain, its causes and effects.

Jillian Powell, *Oil Spills.* Mankato, MN: Bridgestone Books, 2002. Read about one devastating type of water pollution.

Web Site

EPA Environmental Explorers' Club (www.epa. gov/kids). Use this site to learn about pollution and its effects on air, water, plants, animals, and more. In addition to basic information, the site also includes games, experiments, and art projects.

Index

Picture credits

Cover Image: PhotoDisc
AP/Wide World Photos, 5, 23
Charles Cook/Lonely Planet Images, 17
© CORBIS, 20
© Simon Fraser/Photo Researchers, Inc., 24
© Paul Hardy/CORBIS, 8
© Adam Hart-Davis/Photo Researchers, Inc., 17
  (inset)
© Michael Martin/Photo Researchers, Inc., 28
© Jerry Mason/Photo Researchers, Inc., 34
NASA, 7
PhotoDisc, 14
Photos.com, 28 (inset)
© Roger Ressmeyer/CORBIS, 33
Suzanne Santillan, 11, 19, 37
© Jim Sugar/CORBIS, 27
© Tek Image/Photo Researchers, Inc., 38

About the Author

Kris Hirschmann has written more than one hundred books for children. She is the president of The Wordshop, a business that provides a variety of writing and editorial services. She holds a bachelor's degree in psychology from Dartmouth College in Hanover, New Hampshire. Hirschmann lives just outside Orlando, Florida, with her husband, Michael, and her daughters Nikki and Erika.

363. Hirschmann, Kris,
73   1967-
HIR   Pollution

DATE DUE

363. Hirschmann, Kris,
73   1967-
HIR   Pollution

DATE DUE	BORROWER'S NAME	ROOM NUMBER